World War I
in 50 Events

From the Very Beginning to the Fall of the Central Powers

James Weber

World War I In 50 Events

Copyright © 2015 by James Weber

About the Author:

James Weber is an author and journalist. He has a passion for literature and loves writing about social sciences, focusing on history, economics and politics. His hobbies include rowing, hiking and any other outdoor activity. James is married and has two kids.

Other Books in the *History in 50 Events* Series

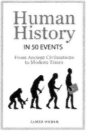  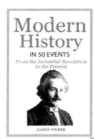 

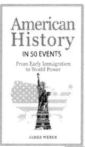  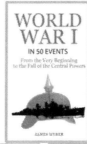 

Table of Contents

Introduction... 9

From the Assassination of Franz Ferdinand to the Battle of Mons 10

1) May 10, 1871 - France Signs Treaty with Germany Ending the Franco-Prussian War.. 11

2) June 15, 1888 - Wilhelm II Becomes German Emperor 12

3) June 28, 1914 - Archduke Franz Ferdinand Is Assassinated....................... 13

4) July 5, 1914 - Kaiser William II Promises Support for Austria against Serbia 15

5) July 28, 1914 - Austria Declares War on Serbia 16

6) August 1, 1914 - Germany Declares War on Russia 18

7) August 3, 1914 - France and Germany Declare War on Each Other......... 19

8) August 4, 1914 - Britain Declares War on Germany.................................. 21

9) August 23, 1914 - Battle of Mons... 22

The War Drags On: From the Russian Defeat at Tannenberg to the British Military Conscription 24

10) August 26, 1914 - Russia's 2nd Army is Defeated in the Battle of Tannenberg... 25

11) September 6, 1914 - First Battle of Marne.. 26

12) October 18, 1914 - First Battle of Ypres.. 28

13) October 29, 1914 - The Ottoman Empire Enters World War I 29

14) January 19, 1915 - First Zeppelin Raid on Britain 30

15) February 19, 1915 - Britain Bombards Turkish forts in the Dardanelles.32

16) April 25, 1915 - Allied Troops Land in Gallipoli 33

17) May 7, 1915 - RMS Lusitania is sunk by a German U-Boat.....................34

18) May 23, 1915 - Italy Declares War on Austria.............................36

19) August 5, 1915 - Warsaw Is Taken By German troops 37

20) September 25, 1915 - Start of the Battle of Loos.........................39

21) January 27, 1916 - Britain Introduces Military Conscription 40

The US Enters the War: From the Battle of Verdun to the Nivelle Offensive

The US Enters the War: From the Battle of Verdun to the Nivelle Offensive **42**

22) February 21, 1916 - Battle of Verdun 43

23) April 29, 1916 - British Forces Surrender at Kut-al-Amara 44

24) May 31, 1916 - Battle of Jutland 45

25) May 31, 1916 - The Brusilov Offensive Begins............................47

26) July 1, 1916 - Start of the Battle of the Somme...........................48

27) December 7, 1916 - Lloyd George Becomes British Prime Minister 49

28) February 1, 1917 - Germany Reintroduces 51

29) April 6, 1917 - US Declares War on Germany.............................52

30) April 20, 1917 - French Nivelle Offensive Fails............................53

The Allies Move Forward: From the Battle of Caporetto to the Turkish Collapse at Megiddo **56**

31) July 31, 1917 - Start of the Third Battle of Ypres.........................57

32) October 24, 1917 - Battle of Caporetto 58

33) November 20, 1917 - British Tanks Win at Cambrai.................................59

34) December 9, 1917 - Britain Captures Jerusalem from the Turks..............61

35) December 15, 1917 - Armistice between Germany and Russia Signed ... 62

36) March 21, 1918 - Operation Michael...63

37) April 3, 1918 - Ferdinand Foch is Appointed Allied Commander 65

38) April 9, 1918 - Germans Begin Offensive in Flanders 66

39) July 15, 1918 - Second Battle of the Marne 67

40) August 8, 1918 - Allies Further Advance in the Battle of Amiens............69

41) September 19, 1918 - Turkish Troops Collapse at Megiddo 70

The Central Powers Surrender: From the Kiel Mutiny to the Treaty of Versailles **72**

42) October 4, 1918 - Germany Seeks Armistice 73

43) October 4, 1918 - The Kiel Mutiny 74

44) October 30, 1918 - Ottoman Empire Signs Peace Treaty.........................75

45) November 3, 1918 - Armistice of Villa Giusti 77

46) November 9, 1918 - Abdication of Kaiser Wilhelm II 78

47) November 9, 1918 - Germany Signs Armistice with the Allies 79

48) January 18, 1919 - Paris Peace Conference 81

49) June 21, 1919 - German Naval Fleet Is Scuttled At Scapa Flow 82

50) June 28, 1919 - Signing of the Treaty of Versailles 83

Introduction

The British Isles have a rich history going back many centuries. The islands were first inhabited by nomads who came from the European mainland, crossing over an ancient land bridge called Doggerland. Footprints of humans found in Norfolk date back over 800,000 years and traces of different tribes suggest first permanent settlements around 500,000 years ago. Until about 14,000 years ago, Great Britain was joined to Ireland, at the same time being connected to the Netherlands and Denmark. Near Bristol, in Cheddar Gorge, the remains of animals native to mainland Europe such as brown bears, antelopes, and wild horses have been dug up alongside those of a human, dated to about 7150 B.C.

During the medieval period, the islands saw several invasions by the Germanic-speaking Saxons, beginning in the 6th century. Over the following centuries, different Anglo-Saxon kingdoms were formed and soon covered most of present-day England. Around the 9th century, Vikings from Norway and Denmark conquered great parts of the country, leaving only the Kingdom of Wessex under Alfred the Great to the Anglo-Saxons.

The Renaissance and Modern periods were marked by major historical events including the English and Scottish Reformation, the Restoration of Charles II, the English Civil War, and the Scottish Enlightenment, as well as the formation of the First British Empire. It was here that the Industrial Revolution first took place and then spread throughout the world.

Today, the British Isles contain two different states: the United Kingdom and the Republic of Ireland. The United Kingdom comprises England, Scotland, Northern Ireland, and Wales, with each country having its own history. (All but Northern Ireland were independent states at one point).

From the Assassination of Franz Ferdinand to the Battle of Mons

James Weber

1) May 10, 1871 - France Signs Treaty with Germany Ending the Franco-Prussian War

World War I arose from growing tensions and difficult alliances throughout Europe. The conflict between Germany and France is considered one of the most important rivalries leading up to the Great War. In 1870-1871, the French fought the (still not unified) German states led by Prussia. Prussian Prince Otto Eduard Leopold von Bismarck had long wanted to create a single German nation and used the conflict to unite the small states and, at the same time, eliminate French influence over Europe. On the other hand, France, under the leadership of Napoleon III, was eager to regain the prestige the country lost after the Vienna Convention in 1815.

French soldiers in the Franco–Prussian War

The German military proved to be the more powerful, and in the Treaty of Frankfurt, signed on May 10, 1871, France agreed to a German occupation and reparation pay of five billion gold francs. This obligation was abandoned in 1873, the same year the German occupation ended. At the same time, Prussian King William I was crowned German Kaiser and went on to unify most of the German speaking states into the German Empire. This new and growing nation concerned many of its neighbors and even the British Empire, which feared new conflicts on the continent. Even though it would take many years for these tensions to explode into the First World War, most of the underlying problems were already visible.

2) June 15, 1888 -
Wilhelm II Becomes German Emperor

As one of the most recognizable German public figures, even today, Wilhelm II would go on to play a major role in World War I. Born in Potsdam, Germany, in 1859, he was the son of Prince Friedrich Wilhelm of Prussia and Princess Victoria, the oldest daughter of Queen Victoria of England. This made him the queen's first born grandchild. Wilhelm was known for his intelligence as well as his temper. His verbal outbursts and ill-advised newspaper interviews later helped his enemies blame the conflict on him.

Wilhelm and his father in 1862

Historians today still debate about his actual role in the war, as well as his responsibility for its outbreak. While he did not actively seek war and openly held back his generals from deploying German troops in the summer of 1914, he did promise support for Austria in case of war with Russia. Some argue that as the conflict went on, he lost power and his military personnel gained control. In 1918, he was forced to abdicate and spent the rest of his life in exile in the Netherlands.

3) June 28, 1914 -
Archduke Franz Ferdinand Is Assassinated

The monument of Stonehenge is located in Wiltshire, England. Even though all that remains is a ring of large stones set within earthworks, it is one of the most famous ancient sites in the world. Scientists believe Stonehenge was built somewhere around 3000 B.C. - 2000 B.C. An examination using radiocarbon dating suggests that the first stones were raised around 2300 B.C., though other theories state that bluestones might have been brought to the site as early as five thousand years ago. Stonehenge and its surroundings were listed as a UNESCO's World Heritage in 1986. The site is owned by the Crown of England and overseen by English Heritage.

The assassination as illustrated in an Italian newspaper

After being captured, Princip attempted suicide with cyanide and his pistol, but both attempts failed, as he vomited the poison and the gun misfired. Since his age of nineteen years made him too young for the death penalty, he received the maximum sentence of twenty years in prison. Princip was held under harsh conditions with little to no food. Three years after the assassination, he contracted tuberculosis and died on April 28, 1918. His killing led directly to the outbreak of the First World War. When Austria-Hungary issued an ultimatum to the Kingdom of Serbia, which was partially rejected, the kingdom then declared war.

James Weber

4) July 5, 1914 - Kaiser William II Promises Support for Austria against Serbia

Following the assassination of Franz Ferdinand, Kaiser Wilhelm II of Germany promised his country's full support for Austria's actions against Serbia. Only a week after the Archduke's murder, an envoy sent by the Austrian Foreign Ministry would reach Berlin. It carried a letter written by the Austrian high official, Leopold Berchtold, emphasizing the need for action in the difficult Balkans region. To further underline the importance of the situation, a personal note from Emperor Franz Josef to Kaiser Wilhelm was attached. The documents explained the need for Austria-Hungary to build an alliance with Bulgaria instead of Romania, which had previously been favored by Germany as an important ally, since it was close with Serbia and the powerful kingdom in the east everyone feared – Russia.

Kaiser Wilhelm's support of Austria-Hungary had great influence on the development of the war

The letter contained no direct evidence that Austria wanted war, but it stated clearly the desire for immediate action. Berchtold wanted to point out the increasing Serbian and Russian aggression in the region, which he believed could only be stopped by eliminating Serbia and its political power in Eastern Europe. The German pledge marked an important decision, as it later turned a regional war between Austria and Serbia into the First World War. Without the Kaiser's support, the conflict in Eastern Europe might have remained localized.

5) July 28, 1914 - Austria Declares War on Serbia

On July 28, 1914, the Austrian-Hungarian Empire declared war on Serbia, therefore beginning World War I. The tumultuous Balkans region had the Austrians worried long before the Archduke's assassinations. Franz Ferdinand's death was simply the last straw, and shortly after having secured the unconditional support of Germany, a military invasion was on its way. However, there was one ultimatum set by Austria-Hungary on July 23, 1914. It ordered Serbia to end all anti-Austrian propaganda within the country, as well as allow an Austrian investigation into the Archduke's assassination. Even though Serbia officially accepted most of the demands made by Austria-Hungary, on July 25, Austria broke off all diplomatic relations with its neighbor and mobilized its military. This action alerted the Russian government, which itself took the necessary measures to prepare for war.

A German newspaper announcing Germany's military mobilization

During the next days, countries such as Britain and France followed the development in Serbia closely, fearing an all-out war in Europe should Russia intervene. British officials proposed the idea of an international conference seeking a peaceful solution to the conflict. The German government, however, refused this proposal and urged Austria to go ahead with its invasion. This pressure did not come from the Kaiser himself, who although he had promised support in case of war, still sought a diplomatic resolution to the conflict. He was ultimately outmaneuvered by German military and congress leaders who favored war. Days later, Austria-Hungary declared war on Serbia and Russia sent troops to the military districts facing Galicia, its common border with the Austro-Hungarian Empire.

6) August 1, 1914 - Germany Declares War on Russia

Four days after Austria-Hungary declared war on Serbia, Russia and Germany declared war on each other. This decision started what many had feared: a war involving the great powers of Europe. On the same day, Russia's ally, France, ordered a general mobilization. It was now clear that a peaceful agreement could no longer be reached. Before the official declaration of war, Germany had warned Russia, which was at that point only partially mobilized, that further mobilization against Austria meant war with the German Empire. At the same time, Germany began the biggest military mobilization in the country's history. After the Russians refused the demands, war plans for a defeat of the Russian army were implemented.

American cartoon showing the European alliances

In the midst of all this, France, long threatened by its arguably more powerful neighbor Germany, began its own mobilization. It urged Great Britain as part of the Triple Entente alliance to officially state its support.

The British government was initially divided on the matter and declined to do so at first. However, as the British further watched the deployment of German troops, the country moved towards war as well. On August 2, German military units crossed the border to Luxembourg heading towards France. Many of the people in Europe looked forward to the outbreak of the war. Most of them believed that their country would be victorious within a short matter of time.

7) August 3, 1914 - France and Germany Declare War on Each Other

One day after crossing the border of Luxembourg and two days after declaring war on Russia, Germany declared war on France. This was part of a strategy proposed by the former chief of staff of the German army, Alfred von Schlieffen. He assumed that a two-front war against France and Russia was possible, though under certain conditions. One of these conditions was a rapid victory against France to free up troops for the eastern front against Russia. Only hours after the German declaration of war, France declared war against Germany. French troops were ordered to move into the provinces of Alsace and Lorraine, regions that had been forfeited to Germany after the Franco-Prussian War in 1871, which France had lost.

German soldiers on their way to the war front

As the war, which had originally started in Serbia, took over Europe, German troops assembled close to the border of neutral Belgium. As part of the Schlieffen Plan, the neutral country would have to be crossed in order to allow a fast invasion of France. Leading up to the Belgian invasion, Germany had presented Belgian King Albert with an ultimatum in which it demanded free passage. This threat would later unite the British government against Germany. In 1839, Belgium's neutrality had been mandated by a treaty that was set up by the leading European powers Britain, France, and Germany. The imminent violation of this treaty made clear that there was little room for reasoning with the German military. Only hours before Germany's declaration of war on France, the British secretary, Sir Edward Grey, spoke before Parliament. His speech convinced the government and led to Britain's entrance into the war.

8) August 4, 1914 -
Britain Declares War on Germany

Once German troops began crossing the border to Belgium, the focus of the war shifted to London. British pacifists and those against the war now had few arguments to present. The government had promised to intervene if Germany did not respect Belgian neutrality, and was furthermore informally committed to help defend its ally, France, against any aggressor. On the same day, the British ambassador delivered an ultimatum to the German foreign secretary, informing him that the German government had until midnight or Britain would declare war. As no German response reached London that night, Britain officially declared war against the German Empire.

British army volunteers after the declaration of war in 1914

This move surprised and angered the German population, which expected war with their rivals France and Russia, though sought to avoid a conflict with their "racial cousins" across the sea. In the high ranks, however, a rivalry between the two countries had been growing for decades. The German navy envied Britain's control of the oceans and Britain's government increasingly saw the rising German Empire as a threat to Europe. With the declaration of war, the continent was now divided into the Central Powers with Austria-Hungary and Germany (and Turkey some time later) and the so-called Triple Entente with France, the British Empire, France, and Russia. Countries such as Norway, Sweden, and the Netherlands remained neutral.

9) August 23, 1914 - Battle of Mons

The Battle of Mons was the first major battle of the war. Unlike the battles that would follow, it was characterized by fast movement. After German troops invaded Belgium, British troops from the British Expeditionary Force (BEF) had crossed the English Channel on August 14. Their general, Sir John French, then planned to meet up with the French Fifth Army led by General Lanrezac at Charleroi. One week later, the British forces encountered cavalry patrols from the German First Army. Even though General French initially made plans to attack the Germans, British intelligence warned him that the size of the German army was still unknown. He then ordered his men to set up defensive positions near the close Mons Canal.

British troops before the Battle of Mons

Germans troops were shocked when they heard about the British approaching, as they had just fought the French Army in an earlier, but significantly smaller, battle. After a few tactical changes, German general Kluck then decided to take on the British on August 23. His position seemed promising, as his troops outnumbered French's more than 2:1. In total, 160,000 German soldiers with 600 artillery guns fought 70,000 British soldiers with 300 artillery guns. General French, now aware of his disadvantage, ordered his infantry to fire their rifles at a combined speed that gave their enemies the impression of being more heavily armed than they really were. This tactic led to a fall in German morale and more casualties than expected. Though the Germans eventually forced the British to retreat, Kluck could not follow the fleeing troops, as he had to deal with unexpected high casualties amongst his own army.

The War Drags On: From the Russian Defeat at Tannenberg to the British Military Conscription

10) August 26, 1914 - Russia's 2nd Army is Defeated in the Battle of Tannenberg

On August 26, 1914, another important battle emerged, taking place on the Russian-German front in East Prussia. The German 8th Army, led by Paul von Hindenburg and Erich Ludendorff, faced the Russian 2nd Army, under General Aleksandr Samsonov. German military intelligence expected Russia to be able to deploy major parts of its troops only in September of 1914. However, due to early planning, the first two Russian armies were deployed already in the middle of August that year. The 1st Army, with its General Pavel Rennenkampf, moved to the northeast of East Prussia, while Samsonov's 2nd Army advanced into the southwest. Both were supposed to join and encircle the outnumbered German troops.

Russian prisoners after the battle

Before the two Russian armies could meet up, the Germans intercepted wireless messages from Samsonov and Rennenkampf and were able to take the 2nd Army by surprise in an area close to the town of Tannenberg. As the fighting began, the Germans used the Russian strategy and encircled Samsonov's forces. Three days later, his troops began their retreat, though they were cut off by Hindenburg, who ordered his troops to show no mercy. During the morning hours of August 30, after witnessing his army collapse, Samsonov committed suicide by shooting himself in the head. The battle of Tannenberg ended with over 50,000 Russian soldiers dead and about 92,000 taken as prisoners of war.

11) September 6, 1914 - First Battle of Marne

At the beginning of the second month of the war, about 30 miles northeast of Paris, the French 6th Army led by General Michel-Joseph Manoury attacked the German 1st Army. Their encounter marked the beginning of the decisive First Battle of the Marne. After having run over neutral Belgium, the Germans began advancing into northeastern France towards the end of August 1914. As they closed in on Paris, they were spurred on by – sometimes overwhelming – victories which forced five French armies to retreat. Expecting a German attack on the capital, the nervous French government named General Joseph-Simon Gallieni as the military governor of the city. He predicted that if no measures were taken, the Germans could reach Paris in the first week of September. In order to defend the capital, he decided to counter attack the 1st Army and convince Joseph Joffre, the French commander in chief, to spare him Manoury's 6th Army.

French soldiers behind a ditch, waiting for the German troops

In the morning hours of September 6, 150,000 French soldiers attacked the German 1st Army on their right flank. As other German troops turned to meet the attack, they opened a 30-mile-gap in their front. This opportunity was seized by the French, supported by a few British divisions, as they poured into the opening and attacked the German troops. The fighting continued over the following several days. Even though the French Army suffered substantial losses, it was able to hold its ground. Military generals even ordered around 6,000 men to be rushed from Paris in taxis. Towards the end of the battle, the Allies continued to push back the Germans. As they came towards the Aisne River, their enemy began digging himself in, beginning the entrenchment of positions that would last until the end of the war. The Allies' successful effort to stop the German army before Paris made the Battle of Marne one of the most decisive battles throughout the war. The Schlieffen Plan was based on a fast victory against the French, which now seemed impossible.

12) October 18, 1914 - First Battle of Ypres

The First Battle of Ypres was part of the "Race to the Sea," which had both German and Franco-British armies trying to move past the northern flank of their opponents in order to reach the North Sea. It took place in western Belgium during October and November of the first year of war. After the Belgian city of Antwerp was captured by the Germans in the beginning of October, the city's remaining forces withdrew to Ypres, arriving there a week later. They met with French and British troops to stop the German advance. The Germans then prepared for an offensive trying to break the Allied lines while occupying Ypres and close channel ports. This would give them control over much of the outlets to the North Sea.

The village of Langemark, which was destroyed in the battle

Once the battle started, it soon became one of the bloodiest struggles of World War I. Allied forces resisted heavy German attacks, and even sought out their own opportunities to break enemy lines. The fighting continued, though both sides suffered heavy losses, until November 22. As the weather became much colder and winter arrived, the battle was then forced to a halt. There were more and more reports of frostbite cases and the physical toll on the soldiers increased. Many troops stayed in trenches that were sometimes half-full of freezing water.

13) October 29, 1914 -
The Ottoman Empire Enters World War I

Although the Ottoman Empire joined the Central Powers in August 1914, it formally entered World War I only in late October, with the bombing of Russian ports in the Black Sea. Following the attacks, the Allied Powers declared war on the Ottoman Empire on November 4, 1914. Historians agree that two major factors led to the Turks entering the war on the side of the Central Powers. As one factor, German diplomatic pressure rose after the war began. German military generals such as Liman von Sanders had renewed and organized the Turkish army and navy in 1913, strengthening the Turco-German Alliance.

Enver Pasha, who played a decisive role in the Turkish alliance with the Central Powers

On the other side, Turkish minister of war Enver Pasha saw the opportunity of expanding the Empire once the war was over. Early victories by the Germans led him to believe the Central Powers were close to winning. This belief was not shared by all Turkish officials, as the Ottoman ambassador in Paris, Rifat Pasha, argued that Enver largely overestimated the German military power. Nevertheless, the Central Powers seemed to appeal more to the Turkish public than the Allied Powers, who in past years had criticized them for harboring German warships.

14) January 19, 1915 - First Zeppelin Raid on Britain

During the second year of the war, a new technology was introduced. Though airships had been invented long before, their military use only started in World War I. Although not the only raids, the England bombings were the best known during the war. In January 1915, the Germans deployed Zeppelin and Schütte-Lanz airships to drop heavy bombs over major cities. The first British casualties were suffered from an air attack on the cities of Great Yarmouth and King's Lynn on the eastern coast of the island.

The crater of a zeppelin bomb

In total, the German Army Air Services realized over fifty raids on the United Kingdom. The difficult weather conditions and hard to navigate airships made accurate bombing almost impossible. Often, their targets (usually military installations) were missed by miles. Instead, large numbers of civilian casualties made the Zeppelins an object of hatred, and they were soon called baby-killers. This fear among the public caused widespread alarm, leading to the diversion of many resources from the Western Front. Defense measures were taken that would later lead to the creation of the Royal Air Force. In total, the raids killed 557 and injured another 1,358 people. The more than 5,000 bombs that were dropped across Britain also caused millions in damage. As the large, highly in-flammable airships were easy to shoot down, they were exchanged with airplanes later in the war.

15) February 19, 1915 - Britain Bombards Turkish forts in the Dardanelles

The Dardanelles in northwestern Turkey, the narrow strait separating Europe from Asia, was a strategic area of high importance to the Allies, as it displayed the only waterway linking the Mediterranean Sea to the Black Sea. After Turkey entered the war on the side of the Central Powers, the area was controlled by Germany and its allies. This kept the Russian navy from the Allied naval forces and hindered cooperation between their ships. The Allies soon decided to attack the Dardanelles and gain control over the region.

The "HMS Irresistible" sinking after having been abandoned

The British plan was to use naval-only bombardment to destroy the overlooking Turkish fortresses. Even though military personnel advised against this move, Winston Churchill, then Lord of the Admiralty, took the plan to the War Cabinet and was able to get approval. He hoped that the bombardments would knock Turkey out of the war without having to divert soldiers from the battles on the Western Front. The Allies could then open a path to Russia and take on the rest of the Central Powers. However, things did not go as planned. The bombardments had little initial impact, because the Turks knew of the attacks in advance and had made their own preparations. Over the next two months, they managed to sink three ships and damage three more by using hidden mines. The British then called off the naval attacks, and plans for a bigger land invasion were made. Winston Churchill resigned as First Lord of the Admiralty, but continued in the military as a commander of an infantry battalion in France.

16) April 25, 1915 - Allied Troops Land in Gallipoli

A week after the naval attacks on the Dardanelles had ended in failure, the Allies began a land invasion of Gallipoli, a Turkish-controlled Peninsula at the northern side of the Dardanelles. On April 25, Allied forces (including New Zealander and Australian troops) landed on the Gallipoli Peninsula. The invasion was supposed to finally gain ground against the Turks, who many believed to be inferior in every military sense. Once again, the British were proven wrong, as enemy forces met them well-prepared, having long been aware of the possibility of the Dardanelles being the place of an invasion. The Australian and New Zealand troops suffered heavy losses as they fought against some of the best-trained Turkish defenders. At the same time, the British and French could gain little ground and met fierce resistance at their landing spots. Some locations reported up to two-thirds casualties.

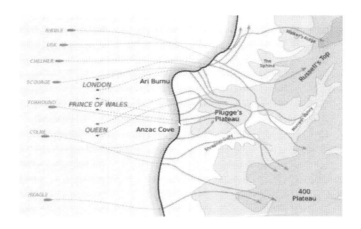

Map of the planned landing on April 25

On August 6, the British landed more troops at Suvla Bay in a second effort to break enemy lines, but failed again. Turkish reinforcements, who quickly dug trenches, stopped their progress. After the British commander Ian Hamilton was replaced by Charles Monro, an evacuation from Gallipoli was ordered. In January 1916, Allied forces were retreated from the peninsula. This marked the end of a disastrous campaign, which resulted in 250,000 Allied deaths.

17) May 7, 1915 - RMS Lusitania is sunk by a German U-Boat

On May 7, 1915, the German U-boat U-20 torpedoed the British ocean liner RMS *Lusitania*, which then sank within 18 minutes. Of the 1,959 people aboard, 1,198 were killed, leaving only 761 survivors. The attack was part of the submarine warfare against the United Kingdom and any of its military ships (the *Lusitania* carried a large quantity of rifle cartridges and non-explosive shell casings). In many countries, the sinking turned public opinion against the Central Powers. In the US, the event was later used as a propaganda symbol in order to recruit troops.

The ship before its sinking in 1907

Earlier attacks on merchant ships in the region prompted the government to warn the *Lusitania* to avoid the south coast of Ireland. Furthermore, it recommended U-Boat evasive actions, such as a zigzag course. The *Lusitania*'s captain ignored these recommendations, as he believed it would negatively affect the passengers' comfort on the ship and delay arrival. In the early afternoon on May 7, the ship was hit on its starboard side by an exploding torpedo. The torpedo caused a second explosion, now believed to be the ship's boilers. Though the *Lusitania* was, in fact, an enemy ship, Germany's action caused widespread outrage, as many of the civilians in the attack were women and children, 128 of them US citizens. Following the sinking, US President Woodrow Wilson received a telegram from his close associate Colonel Edward House, who was in London at the time. House advised Wilson to decide whether

America supported uncivilized warfare or not. He strongly implied that the US could no longer remain a neutral spectator.

18) May 23, 1915 - Italy Declares War on Austria

When war broke out in 1914, the Italian government declared its nation neutral in the conflict, an act that stood against the so-called Triple Alliance, which Italy signed in 1882 and promised support to Germany and Austria-Hungary. During the following months, both the Central Powers and the Allies tried to persuade Italy to join the war on their side. The Italian decision to enter the Allies was largely based on promises made by the British in the Treaty of London, which would hand over large parts of Austria-Hungary after the conflict was won. Italy was even to receive the Albanian port city of Valona, a territory from the Ottoman Empire.

Italian troop climbing the Alps

On May 23, 1915, the day Italy declared war on Austria-Hungary, the declaration opened up a new front in the war. The 400 miles along Italy's border with Austria-Hungary were now potential locations for an invasion. Like Russia, the young Italy was certainly not prepared for industrialized warfare, and many of its soldiers had to be deployed without proper equipment. Nevertheless, the Italian army soon invaded South Tyrol, where it fought Austro-Hungarian troops. The difficult terrain made offensive operations almost impossible, and the initial Italian advance was quickly brought to a halt. Austrians and Italians continued fighting over much of the borderland, with both sides reporting heavy losses. In 1917, German troops that were sent to help Austria-Hungary won over the Italians in the Battle of Caporetto and forced their army to retreat. Despite the Allied victory at the end of the war, many Italians felt betrayed by the British, because Italy was not given all the land promised in the Treaty of London. Some historians argue that this resentment later helped Benito Mussolini into office.

19) August 5, 1915 - Warsaw Is Taken By German troops

During the third battle of Warsaw, also known as the Great Retreat in Russian, the Germans occupied the Polish city of Warsaw following their victory at Gorlice-Tarnow. In the summer of 1915, there was a dispute amongst German generals about to take on the Russian Army. General Ludendorff and General von Hötzendorf were in favor of an encirclement operation, in which the enemy was to be attacked in the extreme northeast and southeast of the salient. General Falkehayn was against this tactic and argued that the Central Powers' poor logistics would force them to move along the railway tracks. Their difference in opinion resulted in a compromise that had the northern half of the troops deployed too far to the southwest to have a real chance of cutting off the escaping Russians. However, this move did directly threaten Warsaw.

Poniatowski Bridge in Warsaw, which was blown up by the Russian Army

As parts of the German army closed in on Warsaw, troops turned north and marched towards the Lublin-Kholm line, which enabled an attack on the city from the east. The first attack on Warsaw began on July 13 and by the end of the week the Germans reached the Narev River. After being held there for a couple of days, the German Army advanced to the Russian fortress of Novo-Georgievsk, on the outskirts of Warsaw. By this time, the Russian commander in chief, Grand Duke Nicholas, ordered to evacuate the city. Soon after, civilians and Russian soldiers pulled out of Warsaw, leaving the capital undefended for the Germans. Nicholas' decision was initially made to avoid unnecessary bloodshed, though inexplicably, the Russians later went on to defend the now useless fortress of Novo-Georgievsk. This fight would cost them more than 90,000 men.

20) September 25, 1915 - Start of the Battle of Loos

On September 25, British troops began an attack on German positions at Loos in Belgium. Their attacks had been prepared by a four-day artillery bombardment along the German front. Part of the plan was to attack the enemy on two sides. While the British proceeded at Loos, French troops would also attack the German lines at Champagne and at Vimy Ridge in of France. The goal was to relieve the suffering Russian Army on the eastern front by forcing German battalions and resources to the western front. The Allies were highly confident about the mission's success due to their superior numbers (in some parts, the ratio to German troops was 3:1). In spite of the numerical strength of the enemy, the Germans successfully defended their positions on both sides. As a defensive measure, they had built a second line of weapons and trenches some miles behind the front lines, which the Allies knew nothing about.

Picture of British soldiers advancing through poisonous gas in September 1915

German casualties after the offensive reached only 60,000, but combined Allied casualties totaled 250,000. Even though the British made heavy use of their new poisonous gas for the first time in the war, the technology proved to be mostly useless, as it failed to reach the enemy's trenches and inflict any serious damage. Commander in chief Sir John French was blamed for the unsuccessful attacks and would later be recalled by King George V. Douglas Haig was to substitute him in his position in December 1915.

21) January 27, 1916 - Britain Introduces Military Conscription

Until 1916, the British Empire had relied on voluntary enlistment or a form of moral conscription named the "Derby Scheme." Towards the third year of the war, heavy casualties demanded a quick change in policy. On January 6, Prime Minister Herbert Asquith introduced the first military conscription in the country's history. The House of Commons later passed the bill on January 27. This step seemed necessary after the recent developments of the war. Although the country was able to rapidly enlist thousands of volunteers during the first months of the war, many of them were neither trained nor suitable for modern warfare. The so-called "Pals battalions," which consisted of men from the same village and similar professional backgrounds, were often not considered actual soldiers. Germany, on the other hand, had already passed a conscription and was able to steadily build up and train its armed forces for the past four decades.

Military Poster after the conscription was enacted

With the conscription passed, everyone in the country was aware that the war was going to be bloodier than expected. Britain had entered the war thinking that its most important role would be providing industrial and economic help to allies. As the conflict went on, this role changed into something much bigger, with almost half of the country's men between 15 and 49 in the military.

The US Enters the War: From the Battle of Verdun to the Nivelle Offensive

James Weber

22) February 21, 1916 - Battle of Verdun

The Battle of Verdun would become the longest single battle of World War I. High casualties and the negative impact the battle had on the French were important reasons for the British initiating the Battle of the Somme, where they sought to take off German pressure on the French. By the beginning of the battle, the war in most of France had settled into slow and bloody trench warfare. As the Germans planned an attack on the city of Verdun, French intelligence warned high military officials, who disregarded the message as unimportant. Forces in the region were then moved to focus on an offensive strategy somewhere else.

A French mortar used in the battle

Once combat began on February 21, both sides fought rigorously. However, German General Falkenhayn's plan was not to take the city quickly, but to bleed the French and decrease their morale. His decision would cost many thousands of lives, both German and French. Within only four days of the first bombardment on the city, the French troops had suffered over 50 percent casualties, with German losses being almost as heavy. After a series of German gains in territory, the battle – like so many others in the war – was brought into a stalemate. Over the next months, the German resources were stretched thinner and thinner, and General Falkenhayn was replaced by the famous Paul von Hindenburg. Nevertheless, the French managed to take back much of the territory won by the Germans. In December 1916, the attacks were called off, and the German soldiers retreated. In total, their death toll was about 140,000, with the French counting 160,000 losses.

23) April 29, 1916 - British Forces Surrender at Kut-al-Amara

In April 1916, the British military would witness the largest surrender of its troops to that time. On April 29, around 13,000 soldiers led by commander Sir Charles Townshend surrendered to the Turkish and German troops in the town of Kut-al-Amara in modern-day Iraq. They withstood almost five months of constant siege by the Central Powers. Before this day, the British had enjoyed great success in Mesopotamia, occupying the province of Basra by late September and planning to move further up the Tigris onto Baghdad. They were ultimately stopped by Turkish troops at Ctesiphon a month later. To their disadvantage, the British troops were made up of mostly Indian troops that had little experience and training. Being unable to continue fighting, they retreated to Kut.

AFTER THE FALL OF KUT: GENERAL TOWNSHEND WITH KHALIL PASHA (on the right).

Turkish troops began attacking the city with the help of German soldiers on December 5. British morale quickly decreased as supplies no longer reached the city and diseases spread. The heavy winter rains also made it difficult to move troops along the river's banks. Every single attempt of the British to confront their enemy proved unsuccessful and resulted in heavy casualties. On April 29, the town fell and General Townshend and all of his more than 10,000 men were taken prisoner.

24) May 31, 1916 - Battle of Jutland

The battle of Jutland was the largest naval battle of World War I. It began around 4 p.m. on May 31, 1916, when a British and a German ship opened fire on each other some 70 miles off the Danish coast. Leading up to the attack, German Naval Admiral Reinhard Scheer ordered his fleet to a waterway just between Denmark and Norway, close to the Jutland Peninsula. Here they would attack the Allies and try to break up the strong British blockade. What Scheer did not realize was that the British knew about his plan. British intelligence had cracked German naval codes and warned every British ship in the area. Furthermore, a fleet of together more than 120 ships made up of destroyers, cruisers, and battleships made its way to meet the Germans.

Two British ships during the battle

Once the British spotted their enemy's warships, the battle began. Unfortunately for the British, some ships were trailing behind, and only half of the entire fleet would arrive in time for the first fights. Within the first hour, two Royal battle cruisers were destroyed, taking with them over 2,000 sailors. The German lost their superiority, however, once the rest of the British fleet arrived. It managed to surround the majority of the German ships and began sinking one after the other. With the inevitable defeat coming closer, German Admiral Scheer decided to withdraw his ships under cover of darkness. This move ended the battle and robbed the British of the possibility to destroy the German navy once and for all.

James Weber

25) May 31, 1916 -
The Brusilov Offensive Begins

The Brusilov Offensive, named after a 63-year-old Russian commander and former cavalryman, went on to become the biggest and most successful Allied offensive of the war. After Russia had suffered great losses during the first two years of the war, attacks on the Germans were now more carefully planned and executed. One of them was to take place in the northern region of the Eastern Front. As part of the attack, Brusilov's troops started bombarding the city of Lutsk along a more than 200-mile-long front. The bombardment was successful and obliterated any advantage the Austrian troops had in terms of numbers. With this strategy, Brusilov was able to overcome the initially 200,000 Austrian soldiers with his 150,000 men, taking more than 26,000 prisoners in just one day.

General Aleksei Brusilov

Continuing to capture vast areas of land, the offensive was ended only in September 1916 due to a shortage in resources. In total, it cost the Austro-Hungarian army almost 1.5 million men and twenty thousand square kilometers of territory. With the Russian revolution taking over the country in 1917, Brusilov and his highly successful campaign were largely forgotten. Nevertheless, his strategic mastermind helped the Allies defeat Austria and left the German Empire almost alone in a war that would go on for another two years.

26) July 1, 1916 -
Start of the Battle of the Somme

The Battle of the Somme was part of an Allied attack against the German lines along the Somme River region of France. To make way for British troops, some 250,000 Allied shells had bombarded German positions the days before. On July 1, more than 100,000 British soldiers were then ordered to leave their trenches, cross the no-man's-land, and attack enemy lines. Allies generals expected the shells to have cleared the way for the infantry. However, a series of heavy German machine guns were still intact and shot anyone closing in on the frontlines. The German defense turned out to be a disaster for British soldiers, with 20,000 of them dying on the first day alone. July 1, 1916, was now officially the heaviest day of casualties in Royal military history.

British soldiers marching to the frontline

The battle would go on for more than four more months, during which the Allies were able to advance only about five miles. After the first disaster, later attacks were smaller and even less effective. It has been estimated that for every 100 yards gained, more than 1,000 Allied soldiers had to die. Towards the end of November, the British called off the Somme offensive after months of fighting. In total, more than 600,000 British and French troops were killed or missing. The German army, despite having held off most of the attacks, also suffered more than 650,000 casualties.

27) December 7, 1916 - Lloyd George Becomes British Prime Minister

On December 7, 1916, after Prime Minister H. H. Asquith resigned, Lloyd George took his place becoming the British Prime Minister during the last half of World War I. In total, he held the position for six years. Born in England to Welsh parents, Lloyd George became a lawyer and later joined the Liberal Party. After the outbreak of the war, he served in the British war cabinet as secretary for wars and minister for munitions.

His coalition with the Conservatives in order for him to succeed Asquith as Prime Minister caused a split in his party from which it never truly recovered.

David Lloyd George in 1915

During the war, Lloyd George was a capable leader, being both bold and aggressive. Due to his character, he often found himself in conflict with Commander Sir Douglas Haig, whom he did not trust. Haig had never been hesitant about sacrificing British soldiers in his battles, a strategy

Lloyd George thought to be barbarous. Himself a great tactician, the new Prime Minister managed to successfully combat the German submarine menace by implementing a new convoy system, which every fleet followed. After the war, he would play an important moderating role in the Paris Peace Conference in 1919 between France's harsh demands and American idealistic proposals made by Woodrow Wilson.

28) February 1, 1917 -
Germany Reintroduces Unrestricted Submarine Warfare

Unrestricted submarine warfare had been banned by the German government in 1915. This was because of a letter written by US President Woodrow Wilson after the British ship *Lusitania* was sunk by a German U-boat, killing 1,201 people, including 128 Americans. The restrictions placed on the German navy, especially the U-boat warfare, persuaded some army generals into wanting to abandon the U-boat program altogether.

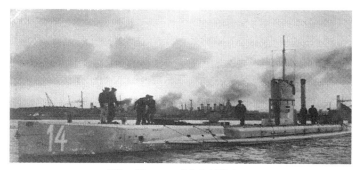

The German U-14 U-boat

The navy commanders, however, were opposed to this degree of passivity. They continued to push for further use of the submarine, even against civil ships. They were able to convince first the army and later Kaiser Wilhelm of the importance of U-boats within the German war strategy and predicted a victory against the British fleet by the end of 1917 if unrestricted submarine use was allowed. With the support of the Kaiser, the navy now sought to bring German chancellor Theobald von Bethmann Hollweg on their side. Hollweg had always been against such military tactics, from a morale standpoint as well as diplomatic. He feared that this could bring the US into the war, which would make a victory almost impossible. Being pressured by the army and the frustrated German public, he eventually accepted the Kaiser's decision and agreed to the change. He then went before the German Reichstag and announced that unrestricted submarine warfare would resume the following day.

29) April 6, 1917 - US Declares War on Germany

After Germany announced the return to unrestricted warfare against all ships that entered the war zone around Britain, neutral or otherwise, many people around the world were outraged. So far, attacks on neutral vessels, and especially American ships, were declared unfortunate mistakes by the German government. Even though the US sought to help its trade partner, England, it was still hesitant to enter the ongoing war. This changed with the sinking of the Lusitania and the announcement of unrestricted warfare. Public opinion in the United States now turned against Germany, and soon, all diplomatic relations with the Central Powers were broken off.

US Congress declaring war on Germany

On February 22, after the American liner *Housatonic* was shot by a German U-boat, Congress passed a bill intended to make the country ready for war. During the next weeks, Germany sunk several more US ships, which prompted Wilson to appear before Congress on April 2 and call for a declaration of war. His request was granted, and on June 26, the first troops reached France for their combat training. America's entrance into the war marked a major turning point and secured the Allied victory. Until the end of the war, more than two million American soldiers were deployed to Western Europe, counting about 50,000 casualties.

30) April 20, 1917 - French Nivelle Offensive Fails

In April 1917, French commander in chief Robert Nivelle ordered one of the largest attacks against the German lines at the Aisne River. His plan was to use fast, almost blitzkrieg-like tactics in order to overrun the

German lines. With support from Canadian and British soldiers, he confidently estimated a breakthrough on the Western Front to occur within the first 48 hours.

After Nivelle received the okay from the military council, British and Canadian troops were ordered to attack around the town of Arras to pull German reserve troops away from targeted area close to the Aisne River.

One of the first tanks to be used in the war

On April 16, the French troops then began their assault on the German positions. However, the German army had been informed about the incoming attack and made necessary preparations to fight off the enemy. Their trenches were dug even deeper and equipped with heavy machine guns, which allowed them to shoot incoming troops from many hundred yards away. It became clear that Nivelle had been overconfident and his expected rate of advance of more than two kilometers per hour was impossible to fulfill. Even the increased use of tanks did not help the Allies after it began to rain and they were stuck in the mud. That day alone, the French suffered 40,000 casualties, a disaster that was comparable to British loss on the first day of the battle of Somme. On April 20, the attacks were called off and Nivelle was dismissed as commander in chief. He was replaced by a more careful Philippe Petain, a war hero of the Verdun resistance.

The Allies Move Forward: From the Battle of Caporetto to the Turkish Collapse at Megiddo

31) July 31, 1917 - Start of the Third Battle of Ypres

As part of a summer offensive and after the failed Nivelle operation, the Allies launch a renewed assault on German lines on July 31. They once again chose the much-contested region near Ypres in Belgium in what would be known as the Third Battle of Ypres (the first and second battles were actually led by the Germans in an effort to break open Allies lines). Now the British troops would take the first step, commanded by Sir Douglas Haig, known for his will to win at all costs. He sought to destroy major German submarine bases on Belgium's north coast and believed that the German army was close to collapsing. One powerful strike, he argued, would mean the Allied victory. He seemed to be right, at least during the first days of fighting, as the Allies made large advances into German territory. During mid-August, however, heavy rains and bad weather cut off the much-needed supplies and slowed further progress.

Battle terrain after being taken by Canadian troops

Haig, seeing the victory closer than ever, replaced some of his generals and ordered to take the ridge of land east of Ypres. Suffering heavy casualties, the Allies eventually managed to occupy the region. As Haig ordered further advance, the morale of his men decreased. With the third battle of Ypres going into its third month, more and more Allied soldiers died. The Germans were able to reinforce their lines with troops from the Eastern Front, where Russia was weakened by internal turmoil. Even though Canadian and British troops "won" the battle on November 6, many historians point to the 310,000 Allied casualties, as opposed to 250,000 on the German side.

32) October 24, 1917 - Battle of Caporetto

The Battle of Caporetto in October 1917 marked one of the greatest wins of the Central powers throughout the war. After the battle, former Italian lines along the northern stretch of the Isonzo River were virtually nonexistent. Leading up to the event, Italy launched eleven attacks on Austrian troops, during which both sides suffered heavy losses and only little ground was won. In summer 1917, with Austria's defense around the city of Gorizia close to collapse, Italian generals were confident enough to finally break enemy lines. After German generals Erich Ludendorff and Paul von Hindenburg heard the news, they immediately sent several of their own divisions to support the Austrians.

German troops after the battle

The Central Powers decided to launch their own attack on Italian positions once the German troops arrived. After Italian commander Cadorna learned about the Austro-German movements, he ordered his men to push back and set up defensive position. Due to bad weather, the Italian troops were not able to follow their orders and failed build a strong defense as fast as Cadorna had hoped. The German troops started bombing their lines on October 24, with heavily armed infantry attacking a few hours later. Grenades and flamethrowers were used to exploit their advantage and to advance quickly. By the end of the day, the Central Powers had pushed back the Italians more than 25 kilometers. Their advance continued until mid-November when they were stopped only 30 kilometers north of Venice.

33) November 20, 1917 - British Tanks Win at Cambrai

After the Somme offensive in 1916 where tanks had been used for the first time, many doubted their effectiveness. The early models were much slower than the ones we know today and more difficult to navigate. Due to only small openings, the soldiers inside could barely see what was going on outside and the enemy soon figured out that this new technology could easily be destroyed by shellfire. Furthermore, the tanks were only able to operate under good weather conditions, with any sort of mud or uneven surface rendering them useless.

British tank after a failed trench crossing

Some British commanders, however, continued to believe in tank warfare and planned to use it during the next attack against the Germans. A dry stretch close to the Belgian border was chosen and preparations were made. In the morning hours of November 20, several infantry and cavalry divisions and almost 500 tanks advanced to the German lines. They were able to force back the German 2nd Army to Cambrai on the same day, showing the tank's full potential. Unfortunately, as the British had failed to send adequate back up for their advancing troops, almost all of their obtained territory was later regained by a German counterattack of nearly twenty divisions. Nonetheless, the attack boosted the tank's reputation as a new weapon, and they would be part of many more offensives.

34) December 9, 1917 -
Britain Captures Jerusalem from the Turks

On December 9, British troops captured the holy city of Jerusalem after only one day of fighting. The Turkish withdrew from the region after the Allied troops, led by General Edmund Allenby, had proven to be the mightier fighting force. While entering the city, officials of Jerusalem offered symbolic keys to the city to nearby British troops. They were under strict command not to destroy any religious buildings or monuments and to respect the local traditions.

General Allenby entering the city on foot

General Allenby was also told not to enter the city on horseback, as Kaiser Wilhelm did in 1898. Furthermore, no Allied flags were flown throughout the city and only Muslim soldiers from India guarded Muslim landmarks. While churches rang their bells in Rome and London to celebrate the peaceful British arrival, troops read the new state of martial law in English, Arabic, French, Russian, Hebrew, and Greek. All inhabitants of the city were promised security and peace, and the success spurred British morale throughout Europe.

35) December 15, 1917 - Armistice between Germany and Russia Signed

Shortly after the communists seized control of the Russian military headquarters at Mogilev, they proclaimed a formal ceasefire between Russia and the Central Powers. This armistice was to take effect immediately and on all battle zones where Russian troops were involved. It was the first step in Vladimir Lenin's plan to bring his country out of poverty, as he saw the war as the biggest obstacle on his way to prosperity. Before the peace negotiations with Germany, foreign affairs minister Leon Trotsky also urged France and Britain to prepare an armistice with the Central Powers. After no response from the Allies reached Moscow, the new government went ahead and made plans for peace with both Germany and Austria, a move both countries appreciated.

Lenin after the revolution

Interestingly, even though Russia had initiated the negotiations, they would lose much of their territory after the truce, one third of its population, and many natural resources. Lenin accepted this "shameful peace," because he believed it was the only way to save the Russian revolution. According to Marxist theory, eventually the entire world would become communist, an argument he used to convince the Soviet congress to sign the treaty.

36) March 21, 1918 - Operation Michael

In spring 1918, the German planned a major offensive against the Allied forces on the Western Front at Somme River. The operation was designed by German chief of the general staff Erich von Ludendorff, and sought to break the enemy lines at the river and then destroy the British and French forces in the region. Attacks began on March 21, with several bombardments of the British defense positions. German troops would then attack the British 5th Army at their weakest point along the river. There, most defensive positions were in bad shape and needed reinforcements.

British troops withdrawing after the German attack

Once the Germans arrived, panic spread among the British troops who had no means of communication with other divisions nor their superiors. That day, the German army made impressive gains in territory and left its enemy in shock. The success, as well as the capture of many bridges across the river, made Ludendorff confident he could continue the attack and reach Paris. He disregarded advice from his colleagues and threw his already tired troops against the villages of Amiens and Arras. Allied troops were ordered to hold their positions at all costs, which they managed to do after German supply lines and transportation started to break down. Ludendorff had to call off the operation on April 5, but he won about 40 miles of enemy territory.

37) April 3, 1918 - Ferdinand Foch is Appointed Allied Commander

On April 3, French general Ferdinand Foch was formally conferred the post of commander in chief of all Allied forces on the Western Front. Leading up to this, the German army's success on the Somme had lessened Allies hopes for a quick victory of the war. Paris was now under constant siege by the Germans and some believed that the French government should abandon the city. The top commanders of the French and British armies then called for a meeting that would decide over their strategy for the next months. They soon ruled to install a united command that would lead troops from both countries. The question remained who could take on such a role.

Ferdinand Foch in 1916

Field Marshal Sir Henry Wilson suggested his friend Ferdinand Foch, a decorated French commander who, after being defeated on the Somme in 1916, once more worked his way up to become chief of the French military staff. Some officials questioned Foch's mental ability to stand the pressure and stress related to such a position. Nevertheless, no one doubted his commitment to the Allies and his strong will to win the war. After being given the position, he went on to play an important role in halting a renewed German advance on Paris during the Second Battle of the Marne. This triumph had him promoted to Marshal of France.

38) April 9, 1918 - Germans Begin Offensive in Flanders

Even though "Operation Michael" was counted as a success for the Germans, it failed to meet its goal of destroying the British Forces on the Western Front. Now, German Generals had to look elsewhere in order to find an adequate location for another attack. Old plans for an offensive in the Flanders region in Belgium were brought up again and seemed promising. In this northern region, the British and Belgian forces were cramped in a small zone, which could easily be captured. Unexpected good weather also favored German operations since it allowed the usually muddy battlefield to dry. For a successful offensive, the Germans would have to cut off British communications with the ports and later bombard the crowded enemy bases.

French troops before the attack

The bombardment opened two days before the attack on April 7. The Germans then broke through several miles of front and were able to dig new trenches up to five miles in. Their initial success only lasted for a few weeks before French reinforcements arrived and brought the offensive to a halt. With soldiers growing tired of the fighting, the operation had to be called off on April 29. Estimates of the casualties vary, with around 110,000 on the German side, 75,000 on the British, and 35,000 on the French.

39) July 15, 1918 - Second Battle of the Marne

The second battle of the Marne would later be known as the final German offensive of World War I. Shortly after the offensive in Flanders, General Erich Ludendorff decided to start a diversionary attack south of Flanders to force Allied troops away. He would then order more than twenty divisions of the German 1st and 3rd Armies to attack the French east of Reims, while his 7th Army attacked to the west of the city. The two attacks were meant to split up all French forces in Flanders, making it easier for the Germans to take the region. Once the Germans began their attack, however, they realized that hundreds of false trenches had been set up. The actual defense was moved further back and suffered no harm from the bombardment the Germans used to weaken the Allied positions.

French machine gun positions waiting for the German attack

German troops had used bombs and gas-shells on empty trenches and walked right into a trap. Once they reached the second Allied front lines, they were shot down by heavily armored French, British, and American soldiers. Overwhelmed and surrounded, the German army suffered heavy casualties from which it would never fully recover. A few days later, the Allies then counter-attacked, ending the battle in a major victory.

40) August 8, 1918 -
Allies Further Advance in the Battle of Amiens

After heavy German losses during the second battle of Marne, the Allies quickly decided to launch several offensive operations against their weakened enemy. At the same time, German generals realized that the tide had turned against them. Many witnessed a rapid decline in morale and could do little to nothing because supplies and backup were not in sight. Crown Prince Rupprecht suggested beginning negotiations, or at least pulling back the troops, but Ludendorff, German commander in chief, refused such measures, not admitting his losses over the last months.

German prisoners of war after the battle

The Allies, now preparing for a fifth year of war, were reluctant about a large decisive blow against the Germans. Instead, a series of smaller attacks were planned to liberate Western Europe step by step. The commander in chief of the Allied forces Foch ordered the attacks to be "precise and with such rapidity that the enemy had no time to recover in between." Commander Philippe Petain of France, John J. Pershing of the United States, and Sir Douglas Haig of Britain accepted his terms, as they would now be able to act more independently. One of the first of these attacks was to take place at Amiens, aimed to take back territory the Germans had won the previous March. Fighting began on August 8, with the British outnumbering the Germans 6:1. By the end of the day, the Allied forces were able to break open the German lines over some fifteen miles, and thousands of German forces surrendered to their enemy.

41) September 19, 1918 - Turkish Troops Collapse at Megiddo

In September 1918, the British planned another offensive against the Turkish positions near Jerusalem. The first of several attacks was to take place at Megiddo, known by many as the city the Battle of Armageddon in the Bible. Even though the Allies were eager to finally break down enemy lines in the region, they had to wait until the arrival of Indian troops to reinforce their divisions after commander General Edmund Allenby had to order many of his men to the Western Front when the Central Powers launched their massive offensive in spring. On September 19, once the Indian troops had finally arrived the bombardment of the Turkish lines began. Several hours later, they executed a classic feint maneuver, in which British generals led the enemy to believe they would send troops up the Jordan Valley, but later changed the movement of the attack to the west and up the coast.

A Turkish convoy, destroyed by the RAF

Taking the Turks by surprise, the maneuver was a smashing success. The city of Megiddo fell on the same day and communication between Turkish and German troops was disrupted by bombing and blocking railways and roads. Over the next days, the British took several thousand Turkish prisoners and watched the remaining soldiers retreat northward and eastward. Allenby, coming prepared, sent his RAF to cut off the fleeing Turks. With Turkish defenses now almost nonexistent, the cities of Beirut and Damascus fell within the next weeks.

The Central Powers Surrender: From the Kiel Mutiny to the Treaty of Versailles

42) October 4, 1918 - Germany Seeks Armistice

In the morning hours of October 4, 1918, Max von Baden, the new German Chancellor, sent a telegraph message to President Woodrow Wilson requesting an armistice between Germany and the Allied powers. Leading up to the request, the German forces on the Western Front had lost more and more territory over the last months and were now held at the famous Hindenburg Line, the last line of defense. Many army generals who had been optimistic about a German win throughout the first years of war now demanded a change in politics.

German General Erich Ludendorff

German General Erich Ludendorff advised Kaiser Wilhelm to seek an immediate armistice based on the conditions President Wilson had presented in his famous 14 Points address in January 1918. Others, such as von Baden, were reluctant, fearing that an immediate call for armistice would weaken the German position in later negotiations over won territory. He famously said that admitting defeat was only possible when Germany had regained at least some ground on the battlefield. However, on October 4, 1918, after it had become obvious that the situation was growing more critical every day, he heeded Ludendorff's advice and telegraphed his request to Washington. The US government responded that it would only deal with a democratic Germany and did not trust any offers or promises made by an effective military dictatorship. Angered by the response, Ludendorff decided that the war was to resume in full force.

43) October 4, 1918 - The Kiel Mutiny

After the initial request for peace failed, the German Admiralty ordered all sailors and navy soldiers to go to sea and launch one final attack against the British fleet. Standing as a prime example of the frustrated mood of many on the side of the Central Powers during the last days of the war, thousands of sailors refused the order and began to mutiny. At that time, most Germans knew that winning the war was impossible and any new attack would mean unnecessary bloodshed. German naval command Reinhardt Scheer, however, was eager to restore the German navy's prestige and ordered his men to initiate a last attack on the British in the North Sea.

Monument in Kiel in remembrance to the sailors' mutiny

He stated that a possible fight to the death would mean a more honorable end to the conflict than any kind of "dishonorable" peace. In his words, their legacy would sow the seed for the next German fleet. Furthermore, he chose not to inform chancellor von Baden about his plans to leave port on October 28. Once his order reached the ports, news of the suicide mission spread and the vast majority of sailors decided to stay on land. Over 1,000 mutineers were then arrested, which left the Imperial Fleet immobilized. The resistance later turned into a rebellion when sailors and industrial workers alike refused to support the continuing war.

44) October 30, 1918 - Ottoman Empire Signs Peace Treaty

The official signing of the armistice treaty between the Allies and the Ottoman Empire took place on October 30, 1918, aboard the British battleship *Agamemnon*. The ship anchored in the port of Mudros, with representatives of Great Britain and the Ottoman Empire on board. Several Turkish statesmen had contacted Britain about the possibility of peace negotiations during the first weeks of October. With the Turkish forces and economy devastated, it had become the obvious next step.

The HMS Agamemnon

When the Ottoman government first spoke to British generals in the region, the British decided to initiate negotiations without their ally France. This move enraged French Prime Minister Georges Clemenceau and would hurt French-British relations over the next years. First peace talks were held in Constantinople and led by the Ottoman Minister of Marine Rauf Bey. The Treaty of Mudros, which was signed the same day, declared that fights would end at noon the following day. Turkey agreed to surrender all their positions and forts, as well as to open the Dardanelle and Bosporus straits. Prisoners of war were to be released and Arab provinces to be evacuated.

45) November 3, 1918 - Armistice of Villa Giusti

On November 3, officials from the Kingdom of Austria-Hungary and Italy signed the Armistice of Villa Giusti, which would end warfare between the two countries on the Italian Front. The armistice was signed outside of Padua in the Veneto in the Villa Giusti, and was to take effect the next day.

Villa Giusti, the location of the signing

After the Battle of Vittorio Veneto, in which the Austrian army was defeated, the Austrian army began deteriorating quickly. By the end of October 1918, it was obvious that the country was in no shape to continue fighting. From October 28 onwards, the kingdom sought to negotiate a truce but was hesitant to sign the text of armistice. As Italian troops advanced to Trento, Udine, and landed in Trieste, the pressure for a decision increased. After Italy threatened to break off the negotiations, the Austrian government decided to spare its soldiers and accept a ceasefire at any cost. The empire's forces stopped fighting on November 3 and Italy annexed the Southern Tyrol.

46) November 9, 1918 - Abdication of Kaiser Wilhelm II

In November 1918, the Kaiser's position became increasingly untenable. Demands for his abdication spread and American President Woodrow Wilson had made it clear early on that peace negotiations were not possible with the Kaiser in office. Not surprisingly, Wilhelm was reluctant to give up his post and favored a different solution, where he would simply lead his troops from the battlefield back to Germany. His own staff advised against such an act, as they could not guarantee his safety, and many soldiers now held serious grudges against their government.

Wilhelm II, Kaiser of Germany

With no options remaining, Kaiser Wilhelm did what he feared most and gave up all his powers before abdicating his position. He later fled with his family to Holland where he lived in exile. In a proclamation later released to the German public, he renounced all his claims to the German throne and any power connected to it. Every officer and soldiers was to be released from his oath of fidelity to the Kaiser. He died in 1941 at the age of 82 of a pulmonary embolus in Doorn. He died only weeks before Nazi Germany would invade the Soviet Union during the early stages of World War II.

47) November 9, 1918 -
Germany Signs Armistice with the Allies

World War I, also called the Great War, ended when Germany signed an armistice agreement on November 9, 1918. The signing took place in a railroad car outside Compiégne, France. In total, the World War I left more than nine million soldiers dead and more than twenty million wounded. Russia, France, Britain, Germany, and Austria-Hungary all lost about a million lives. During and after the war, an estimated five million civilians died from disease and/or starvation.

Representatives of the Allied forces at the signing of the armistice

At the time of the outbreak of the war, most people assumed that their country would win within months. Millions joined the military forces voluntarily and wanted to be part of the war. This sentiment lasted until the end of 1914, when the German Schlieffen Plan failed and it became obvious that fighting would go on for much longer than expected. Other countries such as the Ottoman Empire and Italy later joined the war on both sides, bringing more parts of Europe into the conflict. When Germany officially surrendered, people from all over the world called it the "war to end all wars." Unfortunately, the Treaty of Versailles forced punitive terms on Germany and angered many. Twenty-one years later, this tension would escalate into World War II.

48) January 18, 1919 - Paris Peace Conference

After fighting ended in November 1918, representatives of the nations involved meet again in 1919, as part of the Paris Peace Conference. With officials from Germany excluded from the conference until May, leaders of the victorious Allied powers began drafting what would later become the Versailles Treaty. Throughout the conference, US President Woodrow Wilson tried to uphold his concept of a "peace without victory." He believed that a harsh treatment of Germany would upset its people and cause further problems. On the other side, Prime Ministers David Lloyd George of Britain and Georges Clemenceau of France agreed that only a severe punishment of Germany would ensure its weakness and repay their expenses.

From left to right: David Lloyd George (Britain), Vittorio Emanuele Orlando (Italy), Georges Clemenceau (France), Woodrow Wilson (US)

In the end, Wilson gave in, not wanting to endanger his new project, a worldwide peacekeeping organization called "the League of Nations."

Once representatives from Germany reached the peace conference in May and saw the proposed draft, they were deeply frustrated. Having believed in American promises, they expected nothing like the territory and pay reparations with which they were confronted. Furthermore, the infamous Article 231 put sole blame for the war on their country.

49) June 21, 1919 -
German Naval Fleet Is Scuttled At Scapa Flow

As part of the armistice that ended the World War II in November 1918, the German navy was ordered to hand over its entire naval fleet to the British. On November 21, 1918, some seventy battleships and destroyers reached the Scottish coast, heading towards Rosyth, northwest of Edinburgh. They were told to haul down the German flag and not hoist it again without permission. Since the Allies had not yet agreed upon what to do with the German ships, around 2,000 German caretakers were kept on the ships and supplies for them arrived from Germany every other week. As the months went on, German officers had trouble keeping control of their men, who had nothing to do but keep an eye on the ships.

The German cruisers Frankfurt, Emden, and Bremse

Rumors spread that the Italians and the French wanted some of the ships for themselves, plans of which England did not approve. German navy general Von Reuter then decided to prepare to scuttle his fleet on June 17 and prevent his former enemies from taking it. His order was carried out on June 21 as all of his ships hoisted the German flag and opened their hatches. The men then took to their lifeboats and watched their ships sink into the sea. A few British ships close by tried to stop the scuttling and force German soldiers back on their ships. Newspapers later reported nine Germans killed and sixteen wounded. The British saw the scuttling as a blessing in disguise, since they no longer had to answer the question of how the ships were to be disposed and German officers were now convinced that the stain of defeat had been erased.

50) June 28, 1919 -
Signing of the Treaty of Versailles

The Paris Peace Conference, which began in January 1919, ended with the signing of the Treaty of Versailles on June 28, 1919. Throughout the negotiations, the political wrangling became intense. France's primary objective was to ensure its security. Neighbor Germany had invaded the country four times over the last hundred years, causing great harm on the French people every time. In addition, there were demands for German land and pay. Other nations such as Italy also requested reparation pay and Britain's was eager to ensure being the only sea might over the next decades.

Palace of Versailles, where the treaty was signed

In the final treaty presented, Germany was stripped of about a tenth of its pre-war territory and all of its overseas colonies. Some parts of the country were to be occupied by Allied forces and the size of the German military was to be greatly reduced. Reparation payments were to be transferred annually to the Allies. The Treaty of Versailles was signed five years to the day after Gavrilo Princip killed Archduke Franz Ferdinand and set off the war. In the years to come, anger amongst the German population about the outcome of the war and the Treaty of Versailles grew. Extremists such as Hitler used these emotions to gain support and power. This led almost directly to what the negotiators in Paris had wanted to prevent – another global conflict.

Other Books in the *History in 50 Events* Series

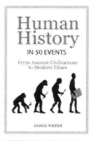

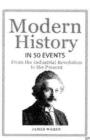

78601253R00049

Made in the USA
San Bernardino, CA
07 June 2018